AUTHENTIC TRANSCRIPTIONS
WITH NOTES AND TABLATURE

DEREK AND THE DOMINOS
LAYLA AND OTHER ASSORTED LOVE SONGS

D1592670

ISBN 978-0-7935-1505-9

HAL•LEONARD®
CORPORATION
7777 W. BLUEMOUND RD. P.O. BOX 13819 MILWAUKEE, WI 53213

EDITOR'S NOTE...

The historic *Layla And Other Assorted Love Songs* album was first released in 1970. Since many of these tunes have become classics in the process of time, in 1990 a 20th-anniversary edition was released called *The Layla Sessions*. Therefore, when we had the opportunity to publish a book of guitar transcriptions of this recording, we had the dilemma of which version to present. Obviously, the Jams from both recordings, plus the Alternate Masters and Outtakes from the *Sessions* album, were too lengthy to include in this collection. So we were left with the 14 "straight ahead" tunes that appear on both the original and anniversary editions.

The main difference between the two recordings is the digital remix and remastering of all the material on the anniversary edition. Alternate guitar parts and percussion were added in the process. With this in mind, but not forgetting the historic renditions of the original tracks, we did the following:

Most of the transcriptions are from the 20th-anniversary edition. All the original guitar parts are there, as well as guitar parts that were not included in the original mix. Four of the longer tunes — "Layla," "Have You Ever Loved A Woman," "Tell The Truth," and "Key To The Highway" — we took from the original recording in order to present them in their original classic form.

Enjoy,

The Hal Leonard Guitar Editorial Staff

I Looked Away

Words and Music by Eric Clapton and Bobby Whitlock

Chorus
w/Rhy. Fig. 2 simile

* Harmony (cue notes)
out 1st time.

(end Vocal Fig. 1)

Verse

Guitar Solo 1
w/Rhy. Fig. 2 simile

* Use slight vib. on each note
for entire solo section (8 bars)

w/Vocal Fig. 1
Gtr. 2

8

Guitar Solo 2

Bell Bottom Blues

Words and Music by Eric Clapton

die,   it would be in _____ your ___ arms. __

Pre-Chorus
Vcl. Fig. 2

Do you wan-na see me crawl a-cross _ the floor _____ to you?

Do ya wan-na hear me beg you to   take me back, _____   I'd   glad - ly do it be - cause

(end Rhy. Fig. 2)

Chorus

I   don't wan - na   fade   a - way _____   Give ___ me one ___ more day, _

please. I don't want to fade a - way.

In your heart I want to stay.

To Coda ⊕
(end Vcl. Fig. 2)

14

2. See additional lyrics
3. See additional lyrics

* Pinched mute w/thumb of of R.H. - producing semi-harmonics.

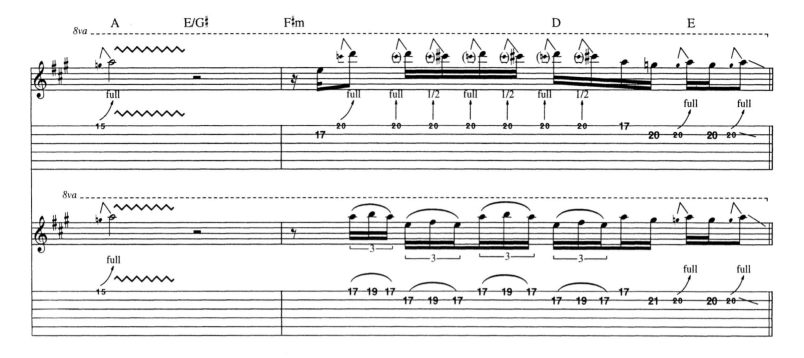

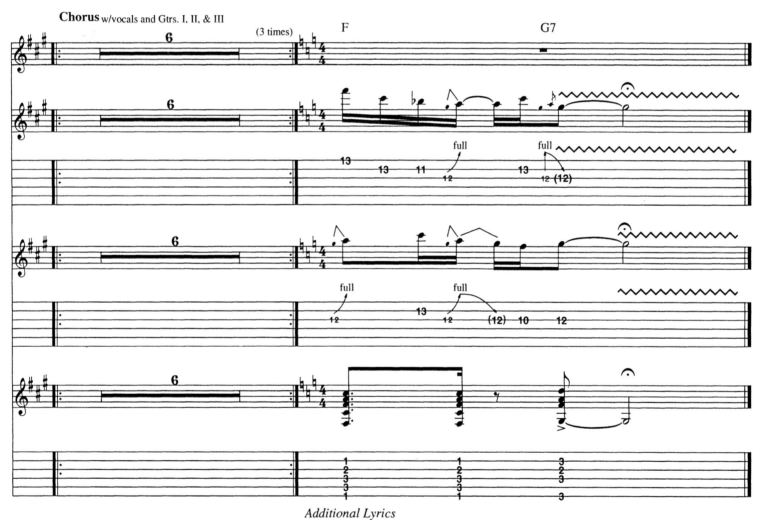

Additional Lyrics

2. It's all wrong, but it's all right
   The way that you treat me baby.
   Once I was strong but I lost the fight;
   You won't find a better loser. *(To Pre-chorus, then Chorus)*

3. Bell Bottom Blues, don't say "Goodbye."
   We're surely gonna meet again.
   And if we do don't ya be surprised.
   If you find me with another lover. *(To Pre-chorus, then Chorus)*

Keep On Growing

Words and Music by Eric Clapton and Bobby Whitlock

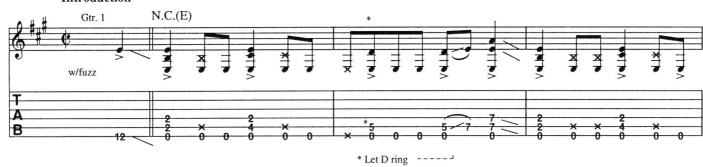

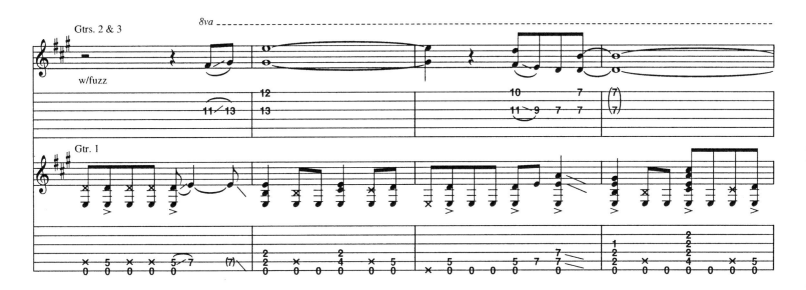

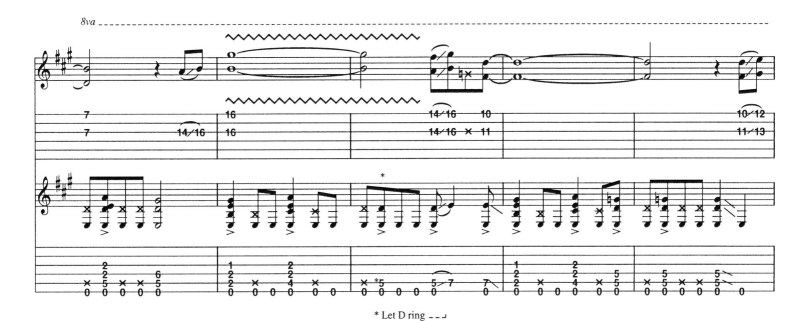

w/Rhy. Fig. 4 & Riff A (simile)

Play - in' _____ the game of love ___ but nev - er real - ly show
Hop - in' _____ and pray - in', Lord _____ that she ___ could un - der - stand _

G5   D/A   A

To Coda I ⊕
To Coda II ⊕ ⊕

- in', _____ I thought that love ___ could wait. _____
___ me, _____ but I did - n't know ___ her name. _____

1st Pre - chorus

E

Rhy. Fig. 5

A

I was a young ___ man and ___ a - sure to go ___ a - stray. _____

1/2

12   12
13   12   14

full   full
10   10 10 10 12   12 (12) 10   10
10   10   11   11
11   11

full
12   (12) 10 10   12   12 (12) 10
full   full

E

D

You walked _ right in - to my life __ and told ___ me,

full   full full full
12 (12)   (12) 17   17   17   17 17 17

23

2nd Pre - chorus (see additional lyrics)

Coda I

w/Vocal Fig. 1
w/Rhy. Fig. 5 simile

* Actual pitch 1/4 below C#

2nd Chorus

grow - in', _____ a - keep on _____ grow - in', ___ a - keep on _____

grow - in', _____ yeah, yeah, __ yeah! _____ (Yeah.) _____

Gtr. 4

Guitar Solo

w/Rhy. Fig. 4 & Riff A - 2 times simile

* Catch F♯ under fretting finger while bending
B♮ (1st stg.), raising it's pitch approx 1/2 step.

N.C.(A)   D/A   (A)   D/A

2/Rhy. Figs. 1, 2, & 3 - 2 times simile

(A)   D/A   G5   D/E   A

(A)   D/A   (A)   D/A

* Actual pitch 1/4 below D♮

3rd Verse

w/Rhy. Fig. 4 & Riff A - 2 times (simile)

Ba - by _____ some - day, ba - by who _____ knows where _____ or when, Lord? _____ Just you wait _____ and see. _____ We'll be walk - ing _____ to - geth - er hand _____ in hand, _____ a - lone _____ for - ev - er, _____ wom - an just you _____ and me. _____

3rd Pre- chorus (see additional lyrics)

Gtr. 4 w/Vocal Fig. 1 & Rhy. Fig. 5 simile

Gtr. 2

Gtr. 3

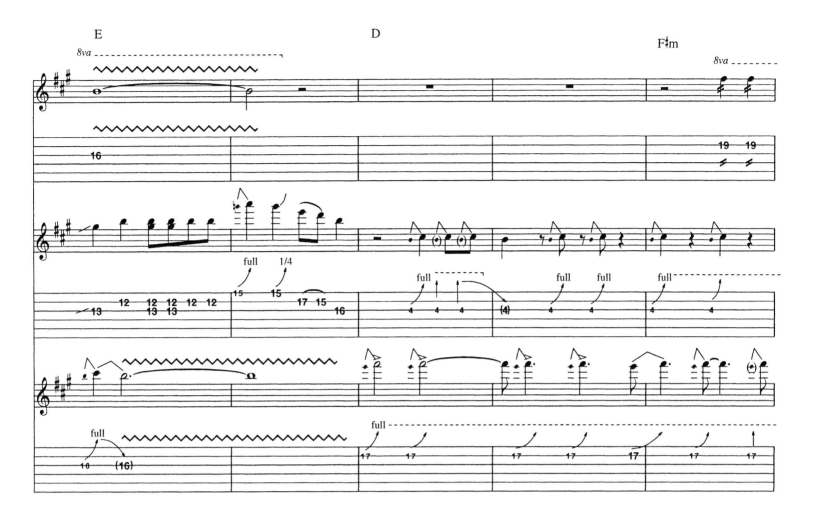

* Actual pitch 1/4 below G♯

* Actual pitch 1/4 above B♮

* Unintentional note

* Finger slide - do not pick

* Actual pitch 1/4 below C#

semi - harm.

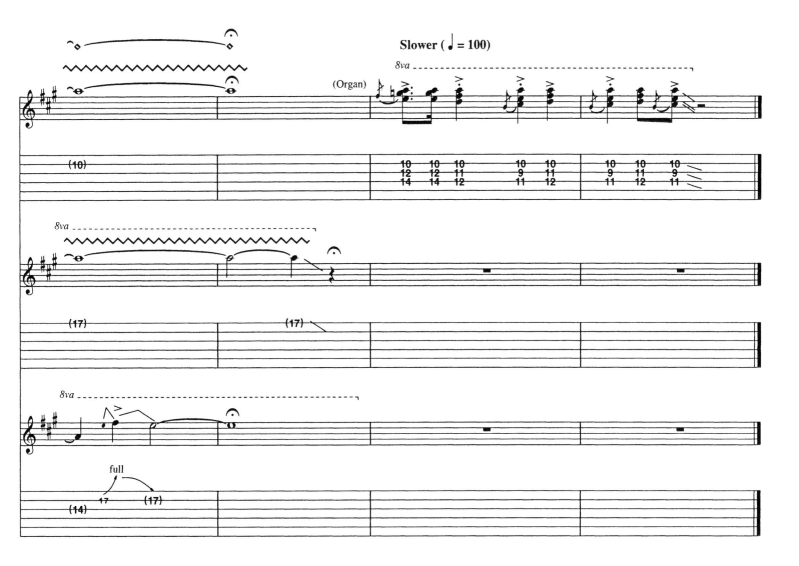

Additional Lyrics

2nd Pre - chorus

> She took my hand in hers
> And told me I was wrong
> She said, "You're gonna be all right, boy
> Whoa, just as long"

3rd Pre - chorus

> 'Cause time's gonna change us, oh
> And I know it's true
> Our love's gonna keep on growin' and growin'
> And here's all we got to do

Nobody Knows You When You're Down And Out

Words and Music by Jimmy Cox

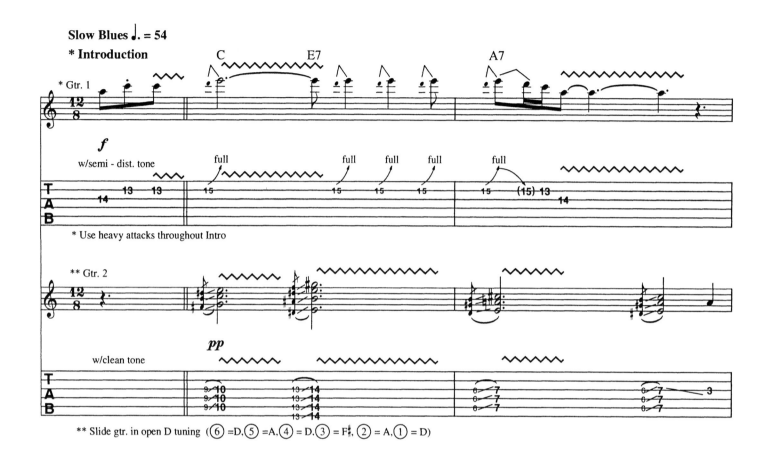

Slow Blues ♩. = 54

* Introduction

* Use heavy attacks throughout Intro

** Slide gtr. in open D tuning (⑥=D, ⑤=A, ④=D, ③=F♯, ②=A, ①=D)

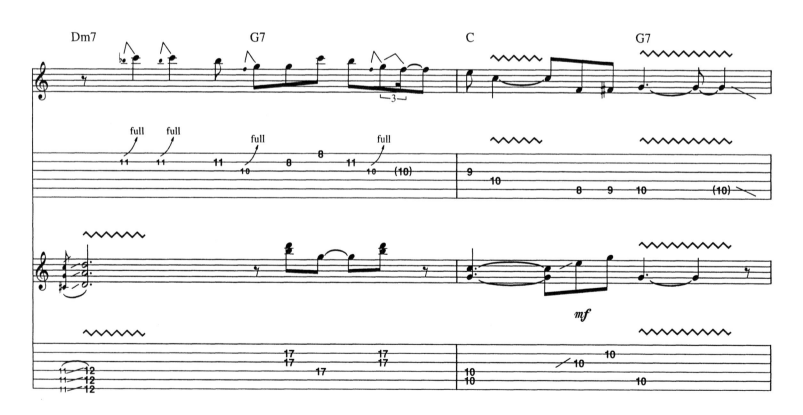

MCA music publishing

* hand slide - do not pick

And when you _ fin - 'lly get   back up - on your _ feet _ a - gain _____

I Am Yours

Words and Music by Eric Clapton and Nizami

but wafts __ your scent __ to me. ___

There sings _ no bird _

but calls __ your __ name __ to me. ___

Each mem -'ry that _

Anyday

Words and Music by Eric Clapton and Bobby Whitlock

*hold 1st note of each rake for full duration of 2nd note of rake

heard you talk - in' and __ I thought __ I heard __ you say _____ yeah, _____

3. *See additional lyrics*

"Please leave me a - lone. ____

Noth - ing in __ this world __ can make __

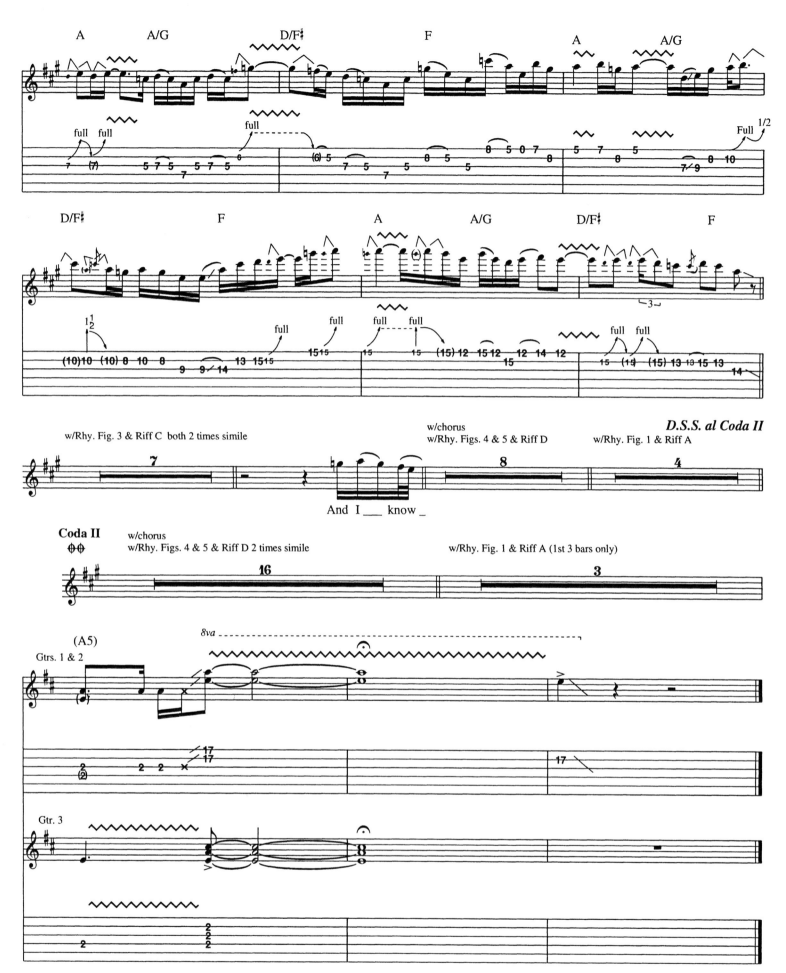

Additional Lyrics

3. Break the glass and twist the knife into yourself.
   Ya gotta be a fool to understand.
   To bring your woman back home after she's left you for another.
   Ya gotta be a - ya gotta be a man. *(To Pre-chorus; then Chorus)*

Key To The Highway

Words and Music by Big Bill Broonzy and Chas. Segar

* open E tuning E B E G# B E

MCA music publishing

* off neck before bridge pick up

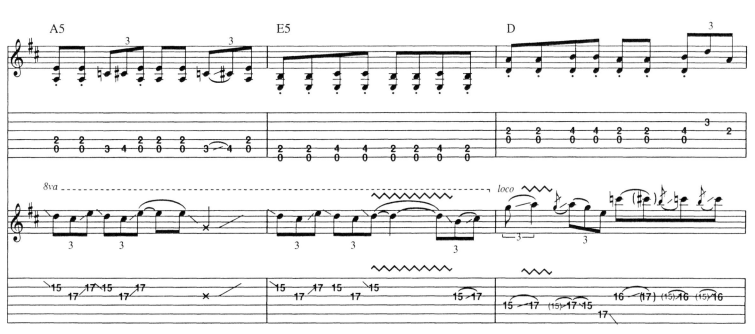

* stg. ③ caught under finger!

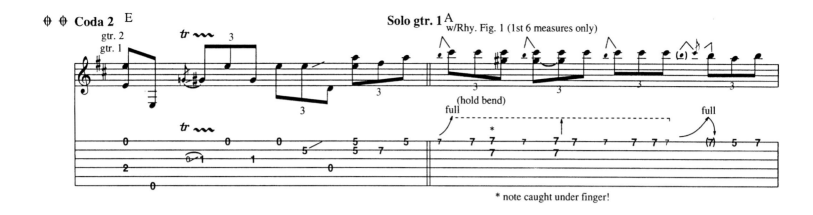

* note caught under finger!

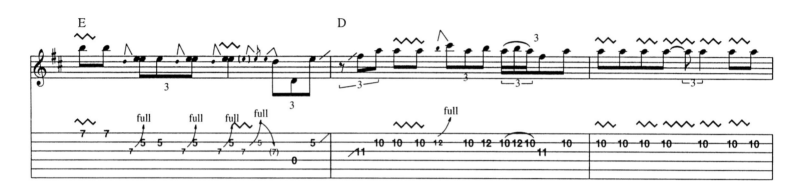

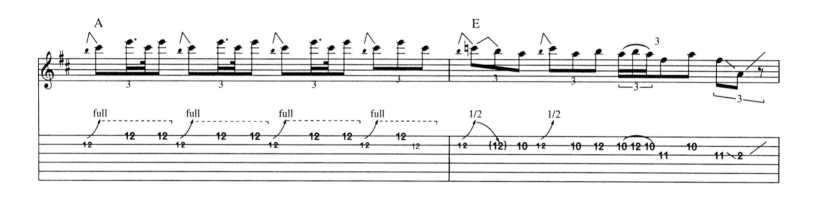

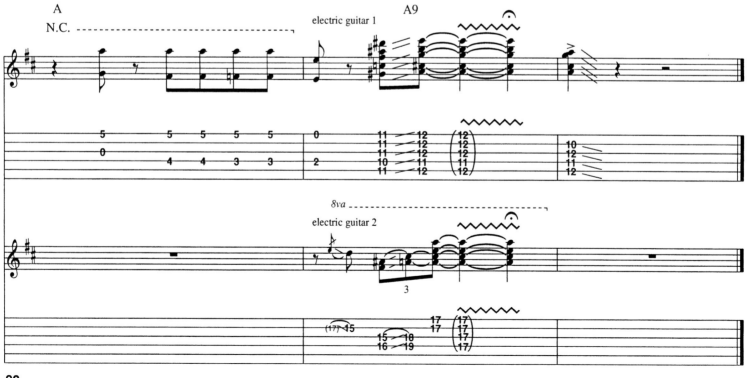

Tell the Truth

Words and Music by Eric Clapton and Bobby Whitlock

oh - oh,   oh

who's been   fool - in'   you, _____   ooh. _____

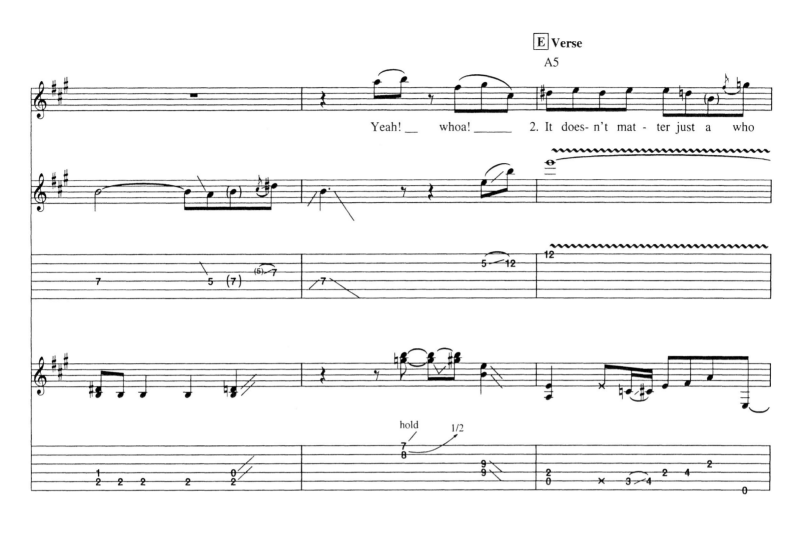

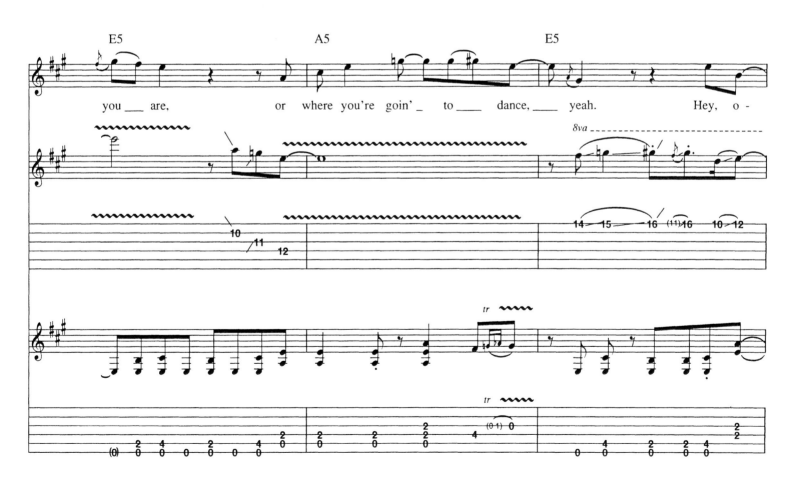

w/Rhy. Fig. 3 (4 times)
Gtr. 2

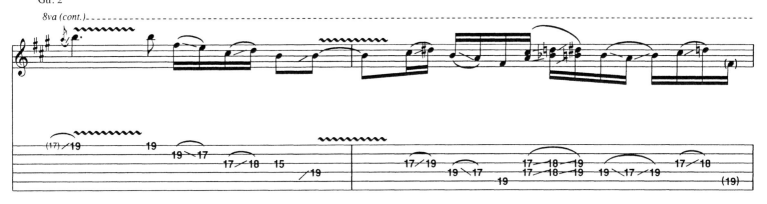

w/Rhy. Fig. 1 (1st 6 measures only)

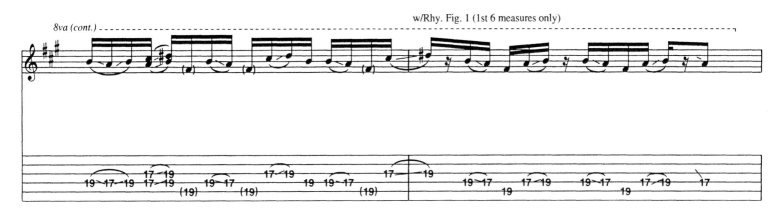

L Outro

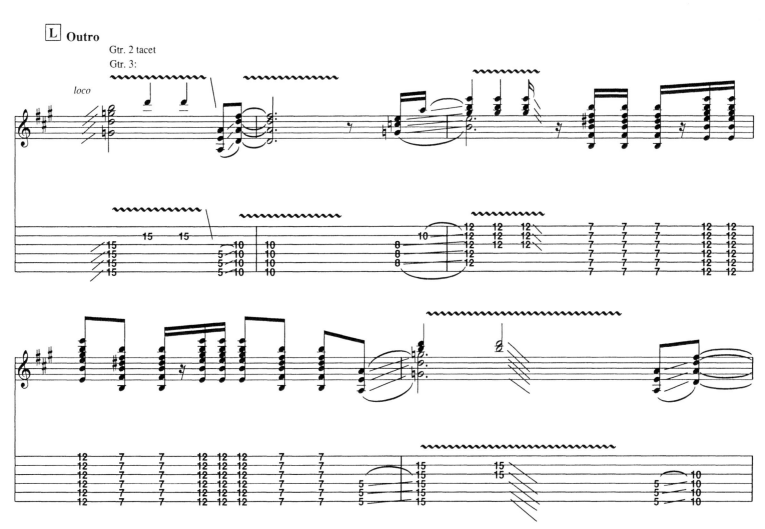

97

Rubato - free time

Why Does Love Got To Be So Sad

Words and Music by Eric Clapton and Bobby Whitlock

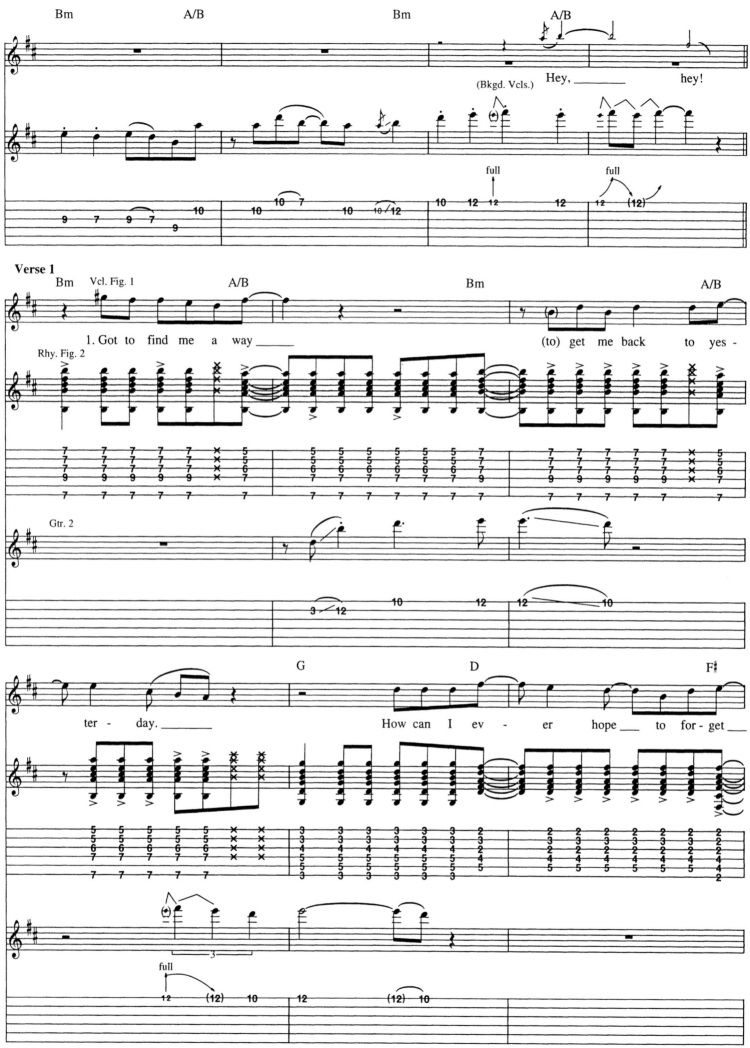

Verse 1

100

* Actual pitch 1/4 below B♮

* Gtr. 4 in cue - notes (up- stemmed noted)

** Gtr. 4 gets lost in mix at this point - 8 bars.

* Vib. refers to both notes of bend.

Verse 3 (*See additional lyrics*)
w/Vocal Fig. 1 cont. Rhy. Fig. 2 simile

Chorus Bmaj7
w/Vocal Fig. 2 - 4 times simile
w/Rhy. Fig. 3 - 18 times simile

109

* Gtr. 4 gets lost in mix at this point.

* Actual pitch 1/4 below D#

* Actual pitch 1/4 below C#

* Strike gtr. body w/pick.

loco

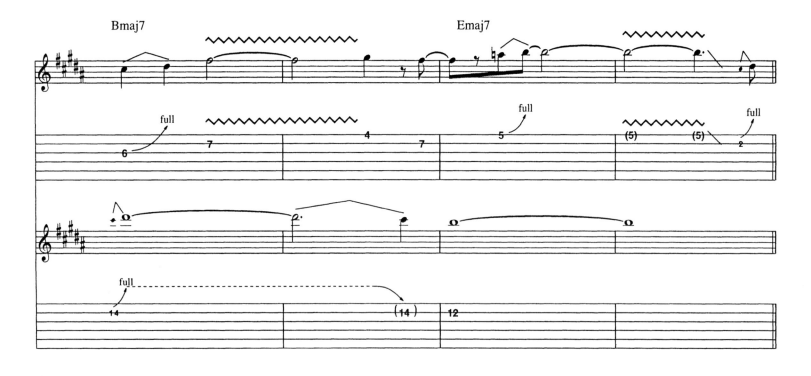

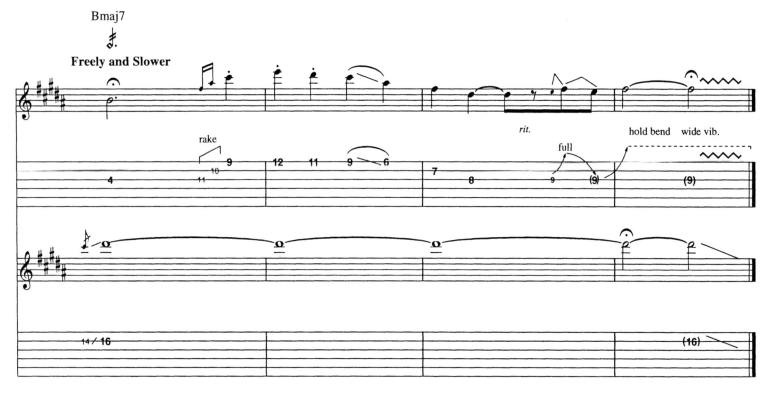

Additional Lyrics

2. Like a moth to a flame,
   Like a song without a name,
   I've never been the same since I met you.
   Like a bird on the wing
   I've got a brand new song to sing.
   Can't keep from singing about you. *(To Chorus)*

3. I'm beginning to see
   What a fool you've made of me.
   I might have to break the law when I find you.
   Stop running away
   I've got a better game to play.
   You know I can't go on living without you. *(To Chorus)*

Have You Ever Loved A Woman

Words and Music by Billy Myles

You just love ___ that wo-man

a yes, _____ so __

much it's a __ shame an' a sin. __

But all the time you know _____ yes, you know, she be-longs ___ to

your ve -ry best friend. _____

C **Guitar Solo**

gtr. 1
gtr. 2 *

* w/slide in open E maj tuning (see pg. 1)

* 3rd stg. caught under finger

* 2nd stg. caught under finger

Some-thin' deep in-side __ o' you   ah, won't let   you wreck ___ your best friend's

home. _____   Oh. _____

Little Wing

Words and Music by Jimi Hendrix

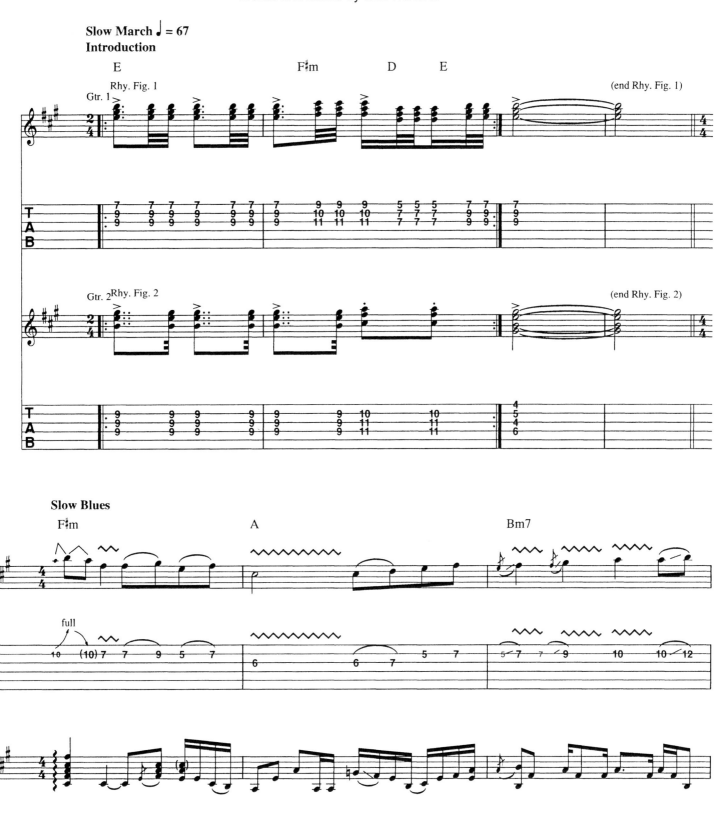

that's all _____ she ev-er thinks __ a-bout.

2. And when I'm sad _____ she comes to me _____

* unintended anticipation

It's Too Late

Words and Music by Chuck Willis

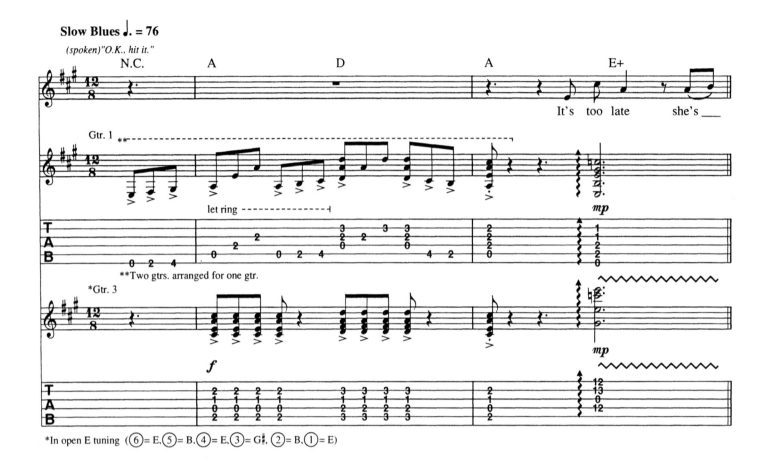

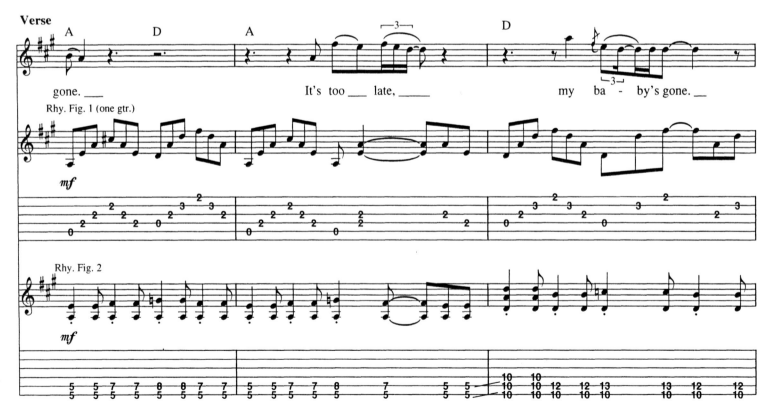

145

Layla

Words and Music by Eric Clapton and Jim Gordon

* Gtr. 1 doubled. The 1st half of the theme is played with conventional fretting
while the 2nd half uses slide. Differences in parts shown in boxed fills.

** Slide gtrs.
Gtr. 3 cont. Rhy. Fig. 1

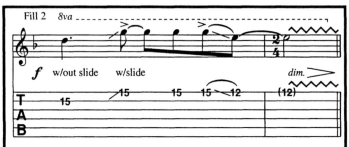

1st Verse

1. (A) what-'ll you do __ when you get lone - ly and no-bod-y's wait-in' by your __

__ side? You been run - nin' and hid - ing much _ too long. ____

la, _____ I beg you dar-lin' please ___ Lay - la, _____

dar-lin' won't you ease my wor-ried mind? _____

Verse

2. I tried to give _ you con - so -la - tion   when your old man, _ he let _ you __

down. __   Like a fool, _____   I   fell in love _ with you, _____

152

Chorus

w/Rhy. Fig. 1 (8 times)

la, _____ you got me on ___ my knees. ___ Lay -

la, ___ beg you dar - lin', please. ___ Lay - la, ___

Gtr. 1

Gtr. 2 *f*
Divisi

*Gtr. 4

*Gtr. 5
Divisi

* Slide gtrs.

155

dar - lin' won't you ease my wor-ried   mind? _____   Lay -

N.C. (Dm)

la, _____   you   got   me   on __   my   knees. __   Lay -
Lay -   la, _____

*Rhy. Fig. 2

*Rhy. Fig. 2

* Rhy. Fig. 2 includes
  gtrs. 1, 2, 4 and 5.

la, _____   I beg you dar - lin', please. ___ Lay - la, _____

Whoa. ___

dar - lin' won't you ease my ___ wor - ried mind?

Whoa! __

No! _____

No! _____

(end Rhy. Fig. 2)

(end Rhy. Fig. 2)
Pickup to overdubbed
slide gtr. solo - - - - ⌐

Gtr. 6

even gliss.

Slide Guitar Solo

Gtr. 3 w/Rhy. Fig. 1 (8 times)
Gtr. 1, 2, 4, 5 w/Rhy. Fig. 2 (2 times)

N.C. (Dm)

* TAB numbers based on
location of notes beyond fretboard

158

159

* Rhy, Fill 2 -- Play 1st measure of Rhy. Fig. 1 and sustain last eighth note diad.

* Piano part arranged for gtr.
All gtrs. are re-numbered for the remainder of the song.

Piano arr. for gtr. ritards simile

Thorn Tree In The Garden

Words and Music by Bobby Whitlock

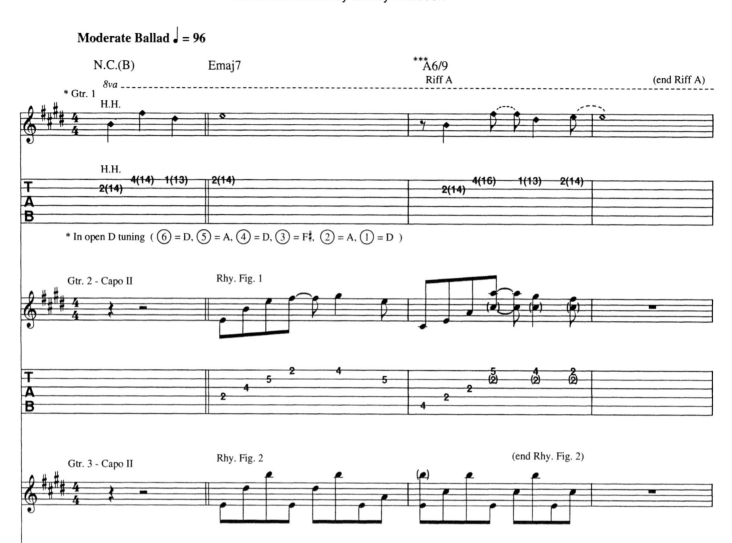

** All open stgs. indicated by fret 2   *** Bass plays E pedal

There's a   thorn tree in the gar - den if you know ___ just what I mean, ___ and I

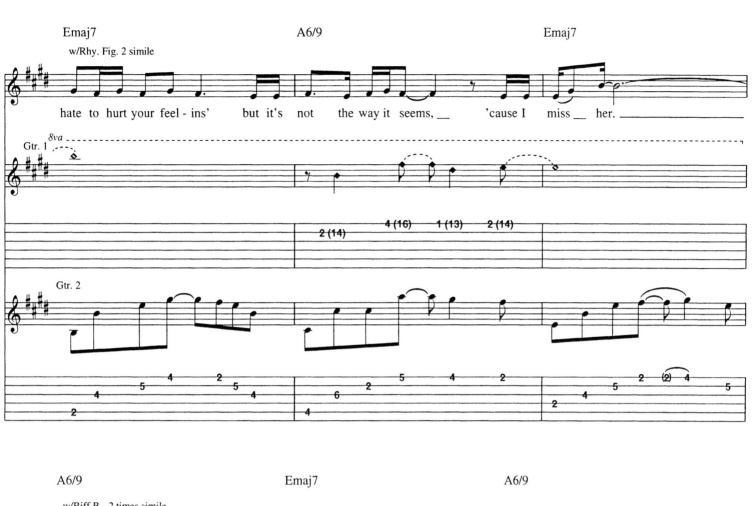

Emaj7   A6/9   Emaj7

w/Rhy. Fig. 2 simile

hate to hurt your feel - ins'   but it's   not   the way it seems, __   'cause I   miss __ her. __

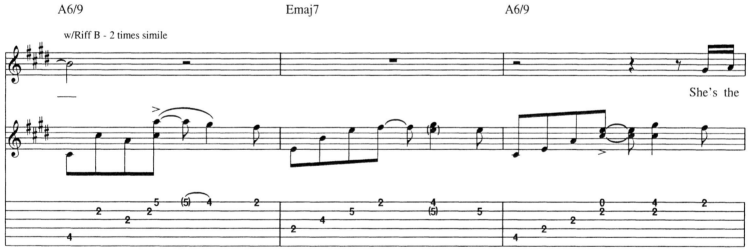

A6/9   Emaj7   A6/9

w/Riff B - 2 times simile

She's the

Emaj7   A6/9   Emaj7

on - ly girl _ I've cared _ for,   the on - ly one I've _ known _____ and   no one ev- er shared _ more love __

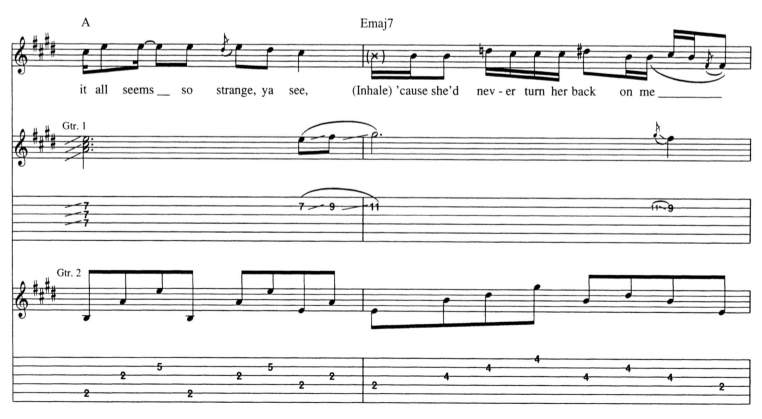

(Inhale) and leave _ with- out ___ a last _ good- bye. __   And if she   winds up walk - in' the streets _

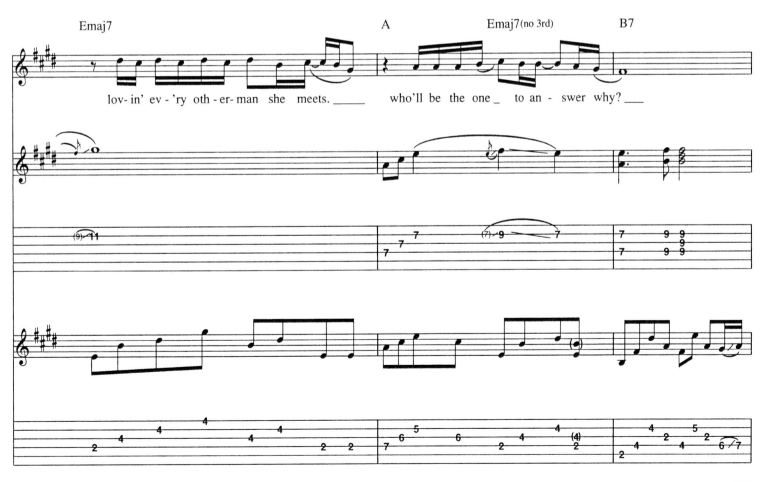

lov- in' ev - 'ry oth - er- man she meets. _____   who'll be the one _ to an - swer why? ___